Where Is Thy Sting?

God's Good Lessons Through Life's Bad Circumstances

A study developed from experiences with God during breast cancer treatment

Michelle O'Toole

Edited by Allison Watkins.

DEDICATION

To all those who stood by me, prayed for me, helped me,
suffered with me, and encouraged me -
may God bless each and every one of you.

CONTENTS

INTRODUCTION

8/9/12

At the suggestion of one of our pastors, I decided to start keeping a journal. "Start" is actually the wrong term, as I have been keeping a journal off and on for the last twenty years of my life. I love journaling. It's a great way to work through my feelings in a place where I can safely say things that probably should never be said aloud. As long as the journal is hidden well, that is! Like taking pictures, it's also a great way to document memories. I love to go back and read about what was going on in my life – all the fun times in my college years, as well as the pain and confusion of my early adulthood.

As I got older and busier, I found less time to write, and over the course of getting married and having four children, I only make the time when I feel like my head might explode. My journal has become a place I only visit once or twice a year maybe, to vent and rant and rave about the difficulties in my life. So, though reading it now tends to make my whole adult life sound miserable, it is safe to assume that every entry that went unwritten was a good day.

Now is a different situation. In the middle of my totally packed, overly busy life, I was diagnosed with breast cancer. That was about two months ago now, and as I lay here in bed, I have nothing but time on my hands. I haven't really felt the urge to write in my journal because I don't have raging fury that I need to let go or awful thoughts to unload on paper.

I have completely been knocked to my knees before the Lord, and now there's nowhere else I can face being. I hesitate to journal because this situation seems so intimate between God and me. I can't figure out if I selfishly want to keep these treasures to myself, or if I can't bear to put the reality of what I am going through into words. Either way, I've always been an open person, and anyone who knows me well would tell you that I love to talk, so I guess if anyone wants to listen, I'll try to write it all down.

ONE

Security in Him

"Surely he will save you from the fowler's snare and from the deadly pestilence. He will cover you with his feathers, and under his wings you will find refuge; his faithfulness will be your shield and rampart" (Psalm 91:3-4).

I guess we need to get caught up to speed. I was going about my business as a mother of four kids, ages eleven, ten, seven and two. I was also working as the children's coordinator at our church part-time. Between sports practices and games, keeping up with the house, doing everything the kids needed for school and working at the church, I was so busy I didn't know which way was up or down. This was fairly new for me, as I had been a stay-at-home mom for the past ten years and pretty much had everything under control. But God provided an opportunity at church that allowed me to stay home with my kids while giving me some much-needed additional income. I have a huge heart for both children and serving, and I was already putting in a lot of volunteer hours, so I really didn't think the position would change my life much.

It was great, but I just couldn't keep up with it all. I would forget it was "Wear a Silly Hat to School Day," or forget I needed to send in special items for a class party. I constantly found myself impatiently telling the kids to hurry up and do their homework, hurry up and eat their dinner, hurry up and get in the car, hurry, hurry, hurry. Thankfully, during this time my relationship with God stayed strong because I felt it was my responsibility as a church staff member to make sure I stayed in-tune with what God wanted, not what I wanted, and to constantly seek Him and follow His lead.

One day, I felt a pain in my left breast. I wasn't feeling well either.

I'd had a cold for several weeks that wouldn't go away, and I was very run-down. I remember having conversations with my husband and my mother about always having pain and never feeling well. I thought everybody felt that way, especially anyone who has a toddler at home. But when my husband told me he never had any pain, a red flag went up for me.

I have always gone to my OB/GYN and done regular self-exams, and I never found anything. But once the pain appeared and seemed to be getting worse, I was able to find what I thought might be a lump, *maybe*. I went to the doctor, and she said it was probably a cyst, but that I needed to get a mammogram. When I got one, they found something suspicious in my other breast as well. They scheduled ultrasounds for both of them.

I really don't remember giving it too much thought. I'm very practical and didn't see any need in worrying when, as of that moment, no one had told me that I had anything to worry about. I also knew that God was in control and that anything that touched me must be ok with Him too.

But as I attempted to go about my normal life, the pain became almost unbearable. I finally had my ultrasound appointment. After the technician finished the ultrasound, she told me that someone, a doctor perhaps (I don't remember), was coming in to talk to me, and she wanted me to "be prepared" that he was going to recommend biopsies. I remember wondering what the big deal was; I had figured they would want to do that next. But she was very serious.

The technician left the room, and as I lay there waiting for the doctor, the scripture we had been working on that month in our children's program came to my mind: "My God is my rock, in whom I take refuge, my shield, and the horn of my salvation" (2 Samuel 22:3). I just kept saying it over and over to myself, and really took it in. *He IS my rock, my everything… everything I base my everything on. He is my refuge, the only one who can provide safe shelter for me… the place where I can go to hide. He is my shield that will go before me and do this for me, with me, ahead of me.* I felt peace. I felt calm and protected.

🕊 **Do you work on scripture memorization?**
   If so, has there been a time it has come to mind
   in a time of need?

The doctor came into the room with the technician, and he told me that both masses looked "suspicious," and he wanted them biopsied. They asked if I had any questions and stood looking at me as if they expected me to burst into tears, or panic, or something; I'm not quite sure.

After the doctor left, the tech asked me why I seemed so calm. I was kind of surprised, as no one had told me that I had cancer or anything, although I knew that was a real possibility. I wish at that moment that I had just blurted out "because my God is my rock, my refuge, my shield…" especially since God calls us to "always be prepared to give an answer to everyone who asks you to give the reason for the hope that you have" (1 Peter 3:15). I dropped the ball on that one. I was not prepared. The words were on the tip of my tongue, and I didn't say them!

That wasn't the first time I've dropped the ball when God gave me an opportunity to witness to others. I want to get good at that. I need to learn to get out of the way and just speak the words that come to my mind. I always pray for opportunities to speak to others about God, but when they arise I seem to chicken out. I have gotten much better lately, after feeling the shame of failing Him in the past.

A couple of years ago in June, my neighbor, whom I didn't know very well but enjoyed chatting with in the driveway every now and then, told me they had found two lumps in her chest, and they thought it was cancer. She looked so sad, so scared. The only words that came to my mind were, "Do you know Jesus?" But I couldn't figure out a way to spit them out of my mouth. I kept thinking I would go over there some other time. I prayed for another opportunity to talk to her.

That December, I sent them a Christmas card and received one back from her husband saying that she had passed away that November. I was shocked that it had happened so fast. I don't know what their beliefs were. I hoped that since he sent me a card with scripture on it, they were believers, but all I knew was that I could never let that happen again. From then on, I was going to speak the words that come into my mind without fear of what people might think.

Now here I am, with another opportunity to tell someone about my God, and I hesitate. I must pray for these opportunities AND have the courage to speak the words He provides. I am working on it. I guess it just takes practice.

1. What does your day-to-day routine look like?

2. God allows all kinds of things to happen in our lives, both good and bad. Does knowing that God has allowed an event affect the way you respond to bad circumstances? How?

3. When you face uncertainties, to whom/what do you automatically turn for security?

4. Read Psalm 18:1-3. List each of the words David used in verse 2 to describe God. For each one, note what mental picture it brings to mind or the meaning it has for you.

5. What does Isaiah 26:4 say about God?

6. Considering all of these descriptions of God, how can they strengthen and reassure you in your times of need?

7. Recall a time when you were in a position to witness to another. Did you speak the word or miss the opportunity? What was the outcome?

8. Everyone needs God. Reread 1 Peter 3:15. What can you do to be better prepared to share God's word with others?

9. How can Paul's instructions in 1 Timothy 4:16 apply to you?

10. Think of people you come across in different areas of your life. Do you see any opportunities to show them who God is? If so, how can you do that?

Extend your study

Mark 16:15

Jeremiah 1:6-8

Notes

TWO

A Heart of Praise

"Do not fear, for I am with you, do not be afraid, for I am your God, I will strengthen you, I will help you, I will uphold you with my victorious right hand" (Isaiah 41:10).

So I went in for my biopsies, waited over a week, and then my husband Sean and I went in for my results. When the doctor walked in, the first thing out of his mouth was, "They're both cancer."

Then he started talking about who knows what, as I literally started laughing and stopped him. I asked if he was kidding, and at the same time, my brain registered that he would never make a joke like that. It was just so strange to hear. I just remember thinking that it was so weird. There is no cancer in my family. I knew after having the tests done that it was a possibility; it just seemed so strange to hear it said to *me*.

Sean and I walked the strangest walk back to the truck. Physically, I felt the same as I did walking in, but now, I could be dying. Nothing really changed except my knowledge.

As I had to make phone calls, telling everyone I had cancer, I did a lot of finding out what I really believed. Strangely, I never cried. I never felt sorry for myself or wondered, "Why me?" Many people told me, "Of all people in the world, this should not be happening to you." But I couldn't help but think, "Why *not* me?" Millions of people go through this, and I'm no different than any of them. I would never wish this on anyone else. I am just a person going through this life with trials and sufferings like anyone else.

I was thankful that this was my diagnosis and not one of my children's. I figured I could do it. *All I have to do is endure the treatments. I can endure.*

8/10/12

Two things were on my mind that I had to deal with: fear of the unknown in terms of the treatment plan, and actually facing what may end up being the death of me.

Let's start with fear of the unknown. There were overwhelming unknowns surrounding my cancer treatment. I didn't realize just how much medical professionals do know about cancer these days. As I've gone from surgeon to oncologist to plastic surgeon to research specialists to navigators to all these people who are here to help, they've each had packets of information for me to read. I had gotten so overwhelmed with information that I couldn't make a decision about anything, and the doctors were leaving the treatment decisions up to me. I just wanted someone to tell me what was best so I could do that. My priority was to survive so my kids could have a mom until they are grown. I didn't care about anything else, like preserving breast tissue and all that, but I guess the doctors give a lot of options because different women in various stages of their lives have different priorities. The only thing I could see clearly was the vision God gave me.

Right after my diagnosis, I saw in my mind a white robe walking in front of me, and I was right behind, clinging to the back of it with both hands. And by "right behind," I mean so close that I had to shuffle my feet as I walked behind it. It is still vividly in my mind and even now, I continue to focus on that, and I know that I'm not going through this alone. What has been really great is that people have been sending me bits of scripture about just that. For example, Deuteronomy 31:8 says, "The Lord himself goes before you and will be with you; he will never leave you nor forsake you. Do not be afraid; do not be discouraged." This is the exact feeling God has been instilling in me, and He has given me that vision to cling to. It's all I have, and all I need.

❦ Can you think of a time when God gave you just what you needed right when you needed it?

I feel so blessed that He has made His presence so known to me. It's a strange way to feel, in the middle of what should feel like crisis. Psalm 63:4-8 is such a favorite of mine right now: "I will praise you as long as I live, and in your name I will lift up my hands. My soul will be satisfied as with the richest of foods; with singing lips my mouth will praise you. On my bed I remember you; I think of you through the watches of the night. Because you are my help, I sing in the shadow of your wings. My soul clings to you; your right hand upholds me."

Many friends have been sending me verses of encouragement, and they really are building me up. It just reinforces that God will stay in this with me. It is all in His hands, and I just have to stick close.

1. Consider Deuteronomy 1:29-31. How did God care for the Israelites on their journey?

2. Can you think of a time when God has fought a fight for you? Carried you? If so, what was the situation? How did it turn out?

3. Have you or someone close to you ever faced a life-threatening situation? If so, how did you handle it?

4. How can you look at challenges in light of Psalm 18:28-29 and Matthew 19:26?

5. Paul says in Philippians 4:4-7 to rejoice always. How can this benefit you?

6. How can this be done in the midst of suffering? See also Psalm 13:5.

7. Paul did not call us to rejoice as one who did not endure life-threatening situations himself. He listed many of his difficulties in 2 Corinthians 11:23-29. Choose the three that stand out to you the most and note them here. As you imagine enduring these hardships, how could having a heart of praise make a difference?

8. Read 2 Corinthians 12:7-10. How could having this outlook change things for you today?

Extend your study

Matthew 5:11-12

THREE

Let Go and Live

"But our citizenship is in heaven. And we eagerly await a Savior from there, the Lord Jesus Christ, who, by the power that enables him to bring everything under his control, will transform our lowly bodies so that they will be like his glorious body" (Philippians 3:20-21).

I talked to my doctors, and we came up with our treatment plan. The plan was to get Adriamycin and Cytoxan once every two weeks for two months, and then Taxol every week for twelve weeks. After that, I will have a double mastectomy. Right now I am in the middle of receiving this treatment. I feel very confident with it. The way I see it is, it's all in God's hands anyway, so with whichever route we choose to take, God will either choose to heal me or not, which brings me to the second issue I have to deal with: death.

I think I've always been a little more comfortable with death than a lot of people. That comes from my practical side, where I am very aware that we are all going to die one day. At any given moment, a car accident, a heart attack, anything can change life in an instant. Sean and I talk about our funeral plans sometimes. For example, I know he wants the bagpipes to play "Danny Boy." His Irish family would be so proud! He knows I want lots of praise songs, like a joyful celebration or a party! But I guess that's a little insensitive. I guess with funerals, you have to walk that fine line between celebrating that the person is with God and consoling those they left behind.

Growing up, I always figured I would end up dying young because I was terribly clumsy. If something could go wrong, it usually did for me. To this day, if there is an exception to the norm, it will happen to me. Sean would agree with this, as he has seen it happen many times.

So I always figured that I'm going to die of something silly, something outrageous. This spring, I injured my toe and it got infected. I actually got a little worried over that because I figured this is just the kind of thing that would kill me! People would be saying, "Poor Michelle's toe infection spread into her bloodstream. Can you believe that? Only Michelle..."

Plus, life can be so hard sometimes that it would just be so much easier to be in Heaven. I just want to serve the Lord, and when He feels I have done all I need to do here, that is great. I can't wait to get to Heaven and see all that He has prepared for us. A lifelong favorite verse of mine is 1 Corinthians 2:9, "No eye has seen, no ear has heard, no mind has conceived what God has prepared for those who love him." I can't wait!

After studying Revelation, I am even more excited to be a part of whatever eternity will be like. I can't wait to see the throne, to see Jesus, to be out of this world of sadness and evil and sickness and pain. Oh, I long for the day of no more tears, of everlasting joy and peace with our Creator. My soul longs for that. But I know that while I am here, I want to serve Him, and I pray that I can be a tool to reach others so that they may share that same eternity. I don't want to hurry out of this place if there is work I can do here. So, I trust God. I trust Him with my mortal life and my eternal life. I figure, whatever happens to me, if it's ok with Him, it's ok with me. Paul's writing in 2 Corinthians 4:16-5:10 speaks on this beautifully:

> Therefore we do not lose heart. Though outwardly we are wasting away, yet inwardly we are being renewed day by day. For our light and momentary troubles are achieving for us an eternal glory that far outweighs them all. So we fix our eyes not on what is seen, but on what is unseen. For what is seen is temporary, but what is unseen is eternal.
>
> Now we know that if the earthly tent we live in is destroyed, we have a building from God, an eternal house

in heaven, not built by human hands. Meanwhile we groan, longing to be clothed with our heavenly dwelling, because when we are clothed, we will not be found naked. For while we are in this tent, we groan and are burdened, because we do not wish to be unclothed but to be clothed with our heavenly dwelling, so that what is mortal may be swallowed up by life. Now it is God who has made us for this very purpose and has given us the Spirit as a deposit, guaranteeing what is to come.

Therefore we are always confident and know that as long as we are at home in the body we are away from the Lord. We live by faith, not by sight. We are confident, I say, and would prefer to be away from the body and at home with the Lord. So we make it our goal to please Him, whether we are at home in the body or away from it. For we must all appear before the judgment seat of Christ, that each one may receive what is due him for the things done while in the body, whether good or bad.

On the other side of this, the selfish part of me wants to stick around here long enough to see my kids to grow into adulthood. I love my little ones, and I do not want them to have to experience the pain of losing a parent. I don't want them to have to grow up missing me and not having a mom. James is only two. He won't even remember having a mom. He won't know how much I adore him. He won't remember reading books and sharing hugs and kisses.

I know I can ask God to let me stay because He tells us to ask for what we desire. But whatever His answer may be, I will be ok with it. If I truly believe that He is protecting my children, which I do, then He will keep them through the time of loss and grieving as well. I believe God will not let me go yet if they will not be ok. So I guess it comes down to trust. Do I really trust Him? Yes.

I called that the selfish part of me, but I don't know. Which one is more selfish? Wanting to be with God in Heaven, or wanting to stay here and raise the children He gave me? Maybe neither? Paul writes about having mixed feelings in Philippians 1:20-24:

> I eagerly expect and hope that I will in no way be ashamed, but will have sufficient courage so that now as always Christ will be exalted in my body, whether by life or by death. For to me, to live is Christ and to die is gain. If I am to go on living in the body, this will mean fruitful labor for me. Yet what shall I choose? I do not know! I am torn between the two: I desire to depart and be with Christ, which is better by far; but it is more necessary for you that I remain in the body.

I guess as long as I am open to either answer from God, I'm not being selfish. Maybe I'm just enjoying the blessings God has given me, yet hopefully awaiting eternity. Maybe that's healthy??

Our pastor was doing a sermon about Esther one Sunday not too long ago, and one verse jumped out of the Bible at me that I LOVE. What a wonderful example for us to follow, and what a wonderful attitude to have. Esther said, "When this is done, I will go to the king, even though it is against the law, and if I perish, I perish" (Esther 4:16b). That's just it, isn't it? We must walk with such faith and be in such close relationship with God that if we perish, we perish, and it is ok.

This whole thing can get really overwhelming, though. I ended up in the hospital last week after a difficult week of side effects. By the time I came home, I was feeling a little defeated. I could also feel fear creeping in, the fear of the pain of death. There were a lot of older people on my floor in the hospital, and I could hear some of them in pain. It was pretty uncomfortable in the hospital with all the constant blood drawing and the feeling of a complete lack of control over what was happening to me. I had a terrible experience with a phlebotomist and her lack of cleanliness and adherence proper procedure, so I followed her down the hall to see if other patients were having the same experience as me. When I saw that they were, I grabbed a doctor on the floor and reported her. But that got me thinking about how I was probably one of the few patients well enough to actually get out of bed and follow someone down the hall in order to right a wrong. Most people there are just so helpless.

It got me thinking about the end, whenever that may be. I do think about the cancer coming back later in life, and what the actual end must be like, but I guess God is with us then, too, and He will give us what we need to get through the actual passing. I figure, it doesn't do any good to dwell on such things though. I go back to taking one day at a time.

℣ Have you ever been in a situation where you felt you had no control? What was it?

I can only face one day at a time. If I look at the long road ahead with nine more chemo treatments to go, then surgery, then possibly another reconstructive surgery, it is too overwhelming, especially when you add in back-to-school time, and sports, and holidays… I don't know what any of that will look like, but I do know how I feel today, and what I can accomplish today. That is what I will focus on. I will also prioritize spending time with God. The minute I let Him slip away from me, I start to get weighed down, so lately I've been choosing a book of the Bible that I am not very familiar with and reading it. I'm sure it will make all the difference.

1. What do you think are some common misconceptions people have about heaven? What do you envision when you think of eternity?

2. What do you imagine it would be like to stand in the physical presence of God?

3. How do these scriptures describe eternity?

- Revelation 21:4
- Revelation 21:6-7
- Revelation 22:3-5

4. How can remembering these scriptures help you face your own death?

5. How does it affect the way we cope with the loss of loved ones?

6. How do we know this future is certain? Read Psalm 9:10 and John 14:1-4.

7. God will not abandon you, nor forsake you. Therefore, you can put your trust in Him. You can let go of trying to control everything that happens to you. You can trust Him with your mortal life and your eternal life. You are free to just *live* in Him, no matter the number of days. How can the following verses help you let go?

- Psalm 86:2
- Proverbs 3:5-6
- Romans 15:13

8. Do you think you would live your life differently if you truly viewed each day as potentially your last? If so, what would you do differently?

Extend your study

Job 19:25-27

Revelation 4

Revelation 21:1 – 22:5

Notes

FOUR

Value in Him

"For you created my inmost being; you knit me together in my mother's womb. I praise you because I am fearfully and wonderfully made; your works are wonderful, I know that full well. My frame was not hidden from you when I was made in the secret place. When I was woven together in the depths of the earth, your eyes saw my unformed body. All the days ordained for me were written in your book before one of them came to be" (Psalm 139:13-16).

Note: In addition to keeping a journal, I also posted updates of my progress on the internet for friends and family. This was the best way to keep everyone informed of what was going on. There, I wrote about a lot of things that I did not include in this journal. One thing in particular I wanted to include in this study was the process of losing my hair. I will include those entries here, but note they are out of chronological order with my previous writing. Thanks for indulging me!

5/31/12

They say my hair will start falling out within the next few days when I brush it. It will be totally gone within the next three weeks. That will be interesting.

6/10/12

A lot of people have asked me how I feel about losing my hair, or if that will be the hardest part of all this. I spent some extra time thinking about it last week because I don't really know how I feel about it. I think I'm ok with it. I have definitely accepted it. But it has never been that upsetting yet. Maybe that's because it hasn't happened yet.

I guess, in a way, it doesn't bother me because that would indicate that the chemo is doing something. If it's killing my hair, it's got to be killing the cancer too, right? So I think maybe that's comforting me. I've never liked my hair all that much anyway. Some of those wigs are nicer than any haircut I've ever had.

But I think what it boils down to is this: Recently, I wanted to spend some time in the Bible, so I turned to 1 Peter and this, of all things in the entire Bible, is what I read:

> Your beauty should not come from outward adornment, such as braided hair and the wearing of gold jewelry and fine clothes. Instead, it should be that of your inner self, the unfading beauty of a gentle and quiet spirit, which is of great worth in God's sight. For this is the way the holy women of the past who put their hope in God used to make themselves beautiful (1 Peter 3:3-5a).

I am so thankful that God speaks to us in so many ways to let us know He is here. I know He is walking before me through this because He takes care of me, sees me, and hears me. Hair doesn't matter. It's just hair.

6/19/12

I am finally on the upswing from the last few days of tiredness. Thankfully, this second dose was not as hard on me as the first, but it still took several days for me to come out of the fog. Some of it is "chemo brain" I'm sure, but the anti-nausea meds really make me drowsy. Once I'm not dealing with the nausea, I can come off of those meds and wake up a bit. I have gotten more done today, which always makes me feel better.

My hair is almost gone. I'd give it another day or two. My scalp has been so uncomfortable, and I feel like I'm always covered in hair, so Sean cut it short for me today. Yes, I did say Sean. ☺ I put a few photos up so that I won't shock you with my bald head in a few days.

6/20/12

Well, my cute little haircut was short-lived. We tore up the lake last night in the boat and left a trail of hair behind. When I woke up this morning, it was so patchy that I decided it was time to get rid of it completely. Sean and I buzzed it all off, and I am pleased to find that my head is not quite as huge as I thought it would be. It does need a tan though, so no pics until it gets a little sun. Jimmy told me he likes my haircut. What a good boy. ☺

7/8/12

The last treatment took a little longer to get over, and I'm sure the one this Thursday will be about the same. I guess the effects are kinda cumulative, so each one is a little tougher than the last. On those days when I am in bed, I try to look to the days that I know will come when I feel better and can get out of the house.

Even with all that, it sounds silly to say, but this trial still feels more like a blessing. I will not attempt to list all of the things I have learned or all of the ways God has moved me through this. (I am not strong; He is.) Maybe one day, but for now I will list all the wonderful new things I have experienced without hair:

1. I can ride with my windows down whenever I want!! It doesn't mess up a thing. I can just crank up the A/C and the music and let that wind blow. It's wonderful.
2. I can take a shower and climb straight into bed. No wet hair on the pillow. Again, wonderful.
3. It takes me half as long to get ready to go anywhere. That means I

can sleep in later.

4. Stepping under a ceiling fan is an absolute delight.

I wish in real life these tiny kinds of things would bring such great joy. Hmmm... note to self. I say "real life" because I feel like my life is on hold. It is so strange. But I guess it doesn't get much more real than this!

🕊 **What are some "tiny" things in life that bring you joy?**

9/5/12

I feel sorry for the people who take me to chemo. I take steroids the night before and again in the morning. I am super chatty all the way there, and then I can hardly stay awake on the way back. The neuropathy in my hands and feet seems to keep staying about the same, so I think I will be able to continue my treatments. They need to end soon, though, or I'm going to end up a big muscle-less, hairless blob. Yes, I have been eating well, but I haven't been as active as I'd like because the heat was just so relentless for a while there. And I am clinging to my last few eyelashes and eyebrows. I tell you what; I sure look like a cancer patient! But I don't mind. And I am very blessed that my hubby doesn't mind either.

You know, my prayer over the last few years has just been, "Here I am; send me!" (Isaiah 6:8). I just want to be God's hands and feet, to do His work. Whatever it may be, I am willing. I tend to use the "hands and feet" reference a lot, and I find it strange that they are now such a big focus of this treatment. Each week I have to watch my hands and feet to make sure we don't cause so much nerve damage that I lose my ability to use them. But even if I did lose mine, it wouldn't keep me from being His.

1. In today's society, how much importance is placed on physical appearance?

2. What kind of judgments do people make about others based on the way they look?

3. How do you tend to determine your self-worth? Is it by the amount you can accomplish in a day? How much money you make? Your looks? The kind of car you drive? Why is that?

4. Once you have gotten to know someone, how much do you care about, or even notice, their physical appearance?

5. How important is outward appearance in God's eyes? See 1 Samuel 16:7.

6. What does Proverbs 31:30 say about beauty?

7. According to 1 Timothy 4:8, what has eternal value?

8. Do you spend more time each day focusing on your physical appearance or your heart?

9. Read Genesis 16:13. Has there ever been a time when God showed you He was there with you, that He sees you and hears you? If so, how?

10. Psalm 139:2-4 is a good illustration of how God knows what we are going through each day. How do these verses compare to John 10:27?

11. God sees everything in your life. He knows you like no other, inside and out, and still loves you deeply. What does this mean to you?

12. How can today's scriptures change your self-image? How can we change the way we look at others?

Extend your study

Proverbs 31:10-3

Psalm 139:5-16

FIVE

Finding Rest

"My flesh and my heart may fail, but God is the strength of my heart and my portion forever" (Psalm 73:26).

8/16/12

One thing that has been so predominant in helping me through the cancer process is all of the scripture I have learned working with the kids at church. I previously wrote about one of the memory verses we had been working on (2 Samuel 22:3), and I wanted to share another.

Last summer, I went to a children's camp for the first time in my life. I never went to any camp at all growing up, so the whole experience was new for me. But it was my job, so I went.

Camp turned out to be such a wonderful experience, even for us grown-ups. I learned so much in the adult gatherings that I will never forget. Right now, I often think of the verse that was printed on the back of the T-shirts they gave us: "And my God will meet all your needs according to His glorious riches in Christ Jesus" (Philippians 4:19). I think about it, I claim victory in it, and it brings me joy. It is a reminder of all that He has done, all that He can do, and all that He will continue to do to meet ALL of my needs. I wore that T-shirt to chemo today. I hope others read it. That is one place where people truly need hope.

It's funny; in the past, I've always considered myself to be a quitter. When things get hard, my natural reaction is to give up and walk away. This time, I don't really have a choice. From the beginning, my outlook has been thankful that it is me and not my child, or anyone else for that matter. I figure, I can do this. All I have to do is get up every day and endure it. That is something I can do, and thankfully I have been able to do it with peace, finding much joy in spite of it.

Though I've heard it a million times, this verse keeps coming to me: "Consider it pure joy, my brothers, whenever you face trials of many kinds, because you know that the testing of your faith develops perseverance" (James 1:2-3). The HCSB version uses the word "endurance." I love it because I feel like it validates my joy despite my illness. It lets me know that it's ok to smile and laugh in our room at the oncologist's office when the tone there is so somber. And I could use a good lesson in endurance and perseverance. I'm in a situation that I can't just quit. I can't walk away from this. I have to learn how to see it through to its completion, to stick it out even when I want to run. This verse is just another reminder that God gives us everything we need and uses everything for our good. He has supplied me with everything I need to get through this treatment, and He is using it to teach me things that are good for me. I'm sure He's using it for the good of others as well.

When the going gets tough, do you tend to stick it out or give up and quit?

8/20/12

I've gotten into a bit of a funk these last few days. I feel pretty good on the Taxol. The only issues are that my hands are a little swollen, both my hands and feet are numb and a little tingly, and my legs ache. I have a healthy appetite, but my stomach can't handle what used to be a normal-sized meal for me. This is really only an issue at dinner. Food just seems to sit in my stomach and go nowhere. If I'm not careful, I get nauseous and have to lie down for the rest of the night. I have enough energy to putt around the house and do a load of laundry here and a load of dishes there, but not enough energy to go shopping or do anything that would take several hours.

So, I have basically been confined to the house. Since my hospitalization, I am also paranoid about germs, so I haven't been going out in public if it can be avoided. Sean does the shopping and errand-running, and I don't even go to church anymore because there are too many people. My oncologist told me to avoid sitting in church, but I didn't want to give that up. Well, after spending four days in the hospital away from my family, I have taken what she said more seriously.

I am concerned about the kids starting school next month and all the germs and illnesses they will bring home. School is always full of sick children, and my kids always seem to catch things, too. I am just so worried that they will get sick and I won't be able to be near them. Then they'll spread it to each other, and weeks will go by where I'll have to avoid my children.

I know that Jesus says not to worry; that's why I chose the word "concerned." ☺ Matthew 6:34 says, "Therefore do not worry about tomorrow, for tomorrow will worry about itself. Each day has enough trouble of its own." Ain't that the truth. I feel like all of this boils down to faith. I have to remind myself that if I truly believe that I will come out on the other side of this, that I will be healed whether by miracle or medicine, then I don't really need to worry about the kids and their germs. I will just be as diligent in germ-control as I can and rely on God to protect me from what may enter my home. Worrying about school starting isn't going to do me any good. I have to focus on Jesus more and remember that He is in control.

See, just like I said earlier, when I start to lose focus on that vision of Him walking right in front of me as I cling to the back of His robe, worry and fear set in. I can't afford to allow that to happen. "Come to me, all you who are weary and burdened, and I will give you rest. Take my yoke upon you and learn from me, for I am gentle and humble in heart, and you will find rest for your souls. For my yoke is easy and my burden light" (Matthew 11:28-30).

Oh, how I need rest for my soul. I have been such a grump lately. I think I've taken my own yoke back, and mine is heavy. I have been hot-tempered and maybe a little self-pitying. The kids are trying my patience, but that is to be expected. Summer is almost over, and they need some time away from each other. I haven't been able to get them out swimming as much this summer, so they probably feel almost as cooped up as I do.

I will work on the scripture above. I need a more gentle heart. I need to remember that walking with Jesus will lighten my load. I can't help but think about all He had to face in His life here, yet His yoke and burden were light. Well then, my burden is nothing.

1. Recall a time when you were in a "funk" due to worry or stress. How did you get out of it, or did you?

2. My dad once pointed out to me that people tend to worry so much about things that haven't happened yet, when most of the time, those things don't end up happening anyway. Do you tend to spend more time stressing about what *might* happen, or taking care of issues when they arise? How does this work for you?

3. When we spend too much time worrying about all the "what ifs" in life, where are we putting our focus? Is this where it should be?

4. What good does James 1:2-4 say comes from trials in your life?

5. As you look back over the trials in your life, has God held true to His promise to you in Philippians 4:19? In what ways?

6. What does John 14:27 tell us about God's peace?

7. Jesus wants us to come to Him to find rest for our souls. How can we do this? See Psalm 55:22 and 1 Peter 5:7. What reason is given in verse 7?

8. Psalm 62:1-2 is a wonderful example of the security we have in God. In Him, we can never be shaken. How can you incorporate this into your life and find rest?

Extend your study

1 Corinthians 15:58

Romans 5:1-5

Notes

SIX

Receiving Love

"From the fullness of His grace we have all received one blessing after another" (John 1:16).

9/7/12

Things have been going well. I have found my new normal. On the day of chemo, I am sleepy. The day after, there is no stopping me. I get all kinds of work done around the house. Then gradually over the weekend, I get achy and start to lie around more, so I schedule and plan accordingly. I have been putting on weight pretty quickly over the last few weeks, but the nurses said that is very normal since they pump me full of steroids every week. Hopefully I can keep that from getting out of control. My spirits are back up. I am excited to be reaching the end of my treatments. While I used to dread surgery, God has changed my heart, and now I'm looking forward to it. At least I know that after that, all I have to do is heal. Hopefully I won't need radiation, and we can be done.

The kids are back in school, which helps. They are busy and happy. I'm really enjoying having so much free time to give them the attention they need. I have been focusing on putting down whatever I am doing at the time if they want to talk to me. I know they will be gone off to college in a flash. Also, I'm so thankful for my friends and family who have been bringing me dinners so that I can spend my energy on things other than shopping and cooking, which reminds me of one of the major things God has taught me through cancer:

It is really easy to give. When you know of someone in need, it feels good to be able to do something about it. We have spent a lot of time at church with the kids going over what the Bible says about giving and how to treat others. Jesus says to "Love your neighbor as yourself" (Mark 12:31). Well, how do we love ourselves? When we are sick, we take care of ourselves. When we are hungry, we eat. When we are cold, we throw some more clothes on or cuddle up under a blanket. When we have needs, the first thing we do is to try to meet them. We need to think of others the same way. If someone is in need, we should try to help them as we would ourselves. We are always blessed by this as well, so it is a joy to help others.

Have you ever had to be on the receiving end? I guess I haven't. Sean and I have struggled, as any other family has, in maturing and becoming a family, but we haven't had any major tragedies; our livelihood has never depended on other people. When someone did something nice for me in the past, I always made sure to send a thank-you note, or maybe a gift card to say thanks and try to reciprocate in some way. But when I had to start chemotherapy, I just couldn't do this all on my own. And suddenly there was this gigantic outpouring of help and prayer from everyone we know and love – our church, family, friends and people I don't even know. I have been so blown away that people care so much about me and my family. I tend to be insecure and feel like I annoy people. Silly, I know now, but I can't help it. So when I got sick, God showed me how much I was loved, and I was shocked. Like, I couldn't take it.

It is really easy to think negatively about myself, but when people gathered for a prayer meeting for me and stepped in to regularly clean my house, drive me to my treatments, take care of my kids and bless them with activities to keep them busy, bring dinners, send cards and gifts, take care of my yard, and I could go on and on, there became no denying that people care about me. I want to send a thank-you note for every kind thing someone has done. I want to be able to appropriately thank everyone and pay them back in some way, but I know it is impossible due to the shear amount of help coming in. I had to learn how to just *receive* it. That is hard – hard, hard, hard. I wish I could give something back. I have to remember how I feel about giving and know that others want to give too.

Long before all this, I had a conversation with a friend at church that keeps coming to mind. She was telling me that she found out that someone close to her was in need and didn't tell her. When she found out after the fact, she told him that he was a "blessing-stealer." She said it is a blessing to serve others, and she loves to do it. I think about that and try not to be a blessing-stealer myself. I have learned to just say thank you and accept everyone's kindness. It's like letting go of something, letting go of being in control maybe. I am in need. I do need this help. Without it, I don't know how I would get through each day. All I can do is thank God for these people. I can feel Him taking care of me through them. I think that's why it's so moving. I feel so blessed to have gone through this because God has shown me in tangible ways that He loves me and that He will meet all my needs. Then, He does *more* than that and gives *more* than I need. It is overwhelming, just like being in His presence. He has made it so clear to me that He is right here taking care of me; I can hardly bear it (in a good way). I've had to learn how to accept the outpouring of His blessings through others without being able to repay any of it.

🦋 **Have you ever been a "blessing-stealer" by not sharing your needs with anyone?**

Maybe that's one reason it's hard to receive: We don't feel worthy of receiving something we can't pay back. That is just what we have to do to receive God's gifts of forgiveness, grace and salvation. These are things we can't earn or pay back. Maybe that's why it is so hard for people to turn to God. They just can't face His kindness and love when they feel so unworthy. This scripture is a reminder that He knows us, loves us and understands us, and of course He does; He created us:

The Lord is compassionate and gracious, slow to anger,

abounding in love. He will not always accuse, nor will he harbor his anger forever; he does not treat us as our sins deserve or repay us according to our iniquities. For as high as the heavens are above the earth, so great is his love for those who fear him; as far as the east is from the west, so far has he removed our transgressions from us. As a father has compassion on his children, so the Lord has compassion on those who fear him; for he knows how we are formed, he remembers that we are dust (Psalm 103:8-14).

1. God understands you to the very depth of your being. He formed you. How can remembering this make your relationship with Him more personal, more intimate?

2. Psalm 103:8-14 are a description of God's perfect love. Is there anything you need to change in your relationships with others to be more like this? If so, what needs to change?

3. Is there anything we have done or can do to earn this love? What does Ephesians 2:4-9 say about this?

4. From the passage above, why does it say God saved us?

5. In Mark 12:28-31, Jesus gives us the greatest two commandments. What are they?

6. God has given us the example of what love is, and He has called us to love each other. Do you find it difficult to show love to every person you encounter? In what circumstances has this been difficult? When is do you find it easy?

7. What does John 13:34-35 say comes from loving others?

8. Do you have to "like" people in order to "love" them? Explain.

9. If you have difficulty loving others, God can change your heart if you ask Him. What does 1 Thessalonians 3:12 indicate?

10. Have you ever been the recipient of love from others without being able to repay them? If so, in what ways? How did it affect you?

Extend your study

Ephesians 1:7-8

Leviticus 19:18

James 2:8

Notes

SEVEN

Just Ask

"If you believe, you will receive whatever you ask for in prayer"
(Matthew 21:22).

9/9/12

Another lesson God has taught me through this is to have more faith that when I pray, He just might say, "Yes." I pray a lot. I pray for God's will in all circumstances. I have disobeyed God at times, and I have learned that I never want to walk outside of His will for me again, ever. But in that, I don't think I ask Him for enough sometimes. I know God wants us to come to Him with our requests, needs and even desires. Philippians 4:6 has always reminded me to come boldly before the throne and ask God for what I need, or for what others need: "Do not be anxious about anything, but in everything, by prayer and petition, with thanksgiving, present your requests to God." I think I used to pray with hope that He *might* give me what I was asking Him for, but He has recently taught me to pray and know that He has heard and answered, and that I need to trust that.

I know He hears all my prayers. I know He answers all my prayers according to His will and in His perfect timing. But I never expected to hear Him as directly as I have regarding my cancer. When I was diagnosed, of course the first thing I did was pray for God to heal me. Whether it is through medicine or miracle, I asked Him to please let me come out on the other side of this. I believed that He would allow me to live through this. But sometimes, when the treatments got really hard, and I was feeling very sick, I would begin to pray again, "God please let me live through this." Twice I began to pray this prayer, and twice God interrupted me mid-sentence to tell me "It's already done."

I believe He has already spoken my healing, and all I have to do is wait for its completion. It has been such a gift to have that reassurance. This word from God has given me strength to get through this with hope and peace. I know a lot of people wonder how I am doing so well mentally through this whole thing, but it is because God is just SO present in all of it. He's just blessing me all the way through it. How could anyone wallow in misery when they are experiencing God so closely?

Matthew 7:7-11 beautifully describes how much it pleases God to bless us when we come to Him:

> Ask and it will be given to you; seek and you will find; knock and the door will be opened to you. For everyone who asks receives; he who seeks finds; and to him who knocks, the door will be opened. Which of you, if his son asks for bread, will give him a stone? Or if he asks for a fish, will give him a snake? If you, then, though you are evil, know how to give good gifts to your children, how much more will your Father in heaven give good gifts to those who ask him!

🕊 **What gift have you given to your child or loved one that has brought you the most joy?**

As we grow closer to God, our desires will be more like His desires. He also encourages us not to give up asking. Jesus encourages us in Luke 18:1-8:

> Then Jesus told his disciples a parable to show them that they should always pray and not give up. He said: "In a certain town there was a judge who neither feared God nor

cared about men. And there was a widow in that town who kept coming to him with the plea, 'Grant me justice against my adversary.'

For some time he refused. But finally he said to himself, 'Even though I don't fear God or care about men, yet because this widow keeps bothering me, I will see that she gets justice, so that she won't eventually wear me out with her coming!' "

And the Lord said, "Listen to what the unjust judge says. And will not God bring about justice for his chosen ones, who cry out to him day and night? Will he keep putting them off? I tell you, he will see that they get justice, and quickly. However, when the Son of Man comes, will he find faith on the earth?"

God will not put us off when we cry out to Him. He will come and judge and make everything right. This makes me think about our government and politics and the end times and all that. I need to pray more for bigger-picture things too. I tend to pray the most for the people right around me and about immediate circumstances. I've read a lot of Paul's letters recently, and it always strikes me how much he prays for the churches. I need to pray for our churches more, and for other believers in this country and around the world. There is so much to pray for. We could pray constantly day and night and never cover everything we need to ask God for.

1. What types of things do you pray for the most?

2. When you pray, what kind of answers are you expecting?

3. Do you take time to listen and look for those answers? How?

4. What does James 1:6-8 tell you about our hearts and minds when we pray? Do you find this more easy or difficult? Why?

5. How can you know that God will answer your prayers? (See 1 John 5:14-15.)

6. Do you only pray for needs, or do you ask for your desires as well?

7. What does Psalm 37:3-4 tell you to do?

8. List three things you feel you should spend more time praying about, and focus on adding those in throughout the week as you pray.

Extend your study

1 Thessalonians 5:17

Matthew 6:5-13

EIGHT

Children of God

"And you also were included in Christ when you heard the word of truth, the gospel of your salvation. Having believed, you were marked in him with a seal, the promised Holy Spirit, who is a deposit guaranteeing our inheritance until the redemption of those who are God's possession—to the praise of his glory" (Ephesians 1:13-14).

9/21/12

A close friend shared a devotional with me the other day, and we were chatting about being spirit-filled. A lot of people tell me that they think I'm handling my bout with cancer very well, and that I must be holding things in. I must be putting on a brave face and hiding all of the bad stuff. I'm really not. It's just that God is handling it for me. I have chosen to stay close by Him, to read the Bible, to pray, to worship. To stay immersed, I guess.

All that God has been for me has got me thinking about the Trinity, and how each part has been so important and so apparent and so present in this experience. It feels like the Father has been my protector, my rock, my safety, my reassurance, my comfort. Jesus has been my partner in suffering, my guide, my help, that one walking before me whom I cling to. The Holy Spirit has been my power, my strength, my endurance, my joy, my peace. I don't think I've ever experienced that fullness of God before. If I have, I haven't paid enough attention to notice. Right now He definitely has my attention, and I don't intend to ever go back to the way I was before. I don't think I can, after experiencing this much of God. I will never allow my life to become so full that I do not immerse myself in Him first. What a gift.

I certainly look at life differently now. Things I used to spend so much time worrying about or trying to figure out just aren't important in the whole scheme of life. I will live each day very deliberately from now on, and I will not allow time to pass me by. Even if we live long, full lives, they are very short compared to eternity, and each day must count. Each interaction with every person we pass is important.

From now on, I'm going to speak the words on my heart to people. I'm not going to worry about what people think. That is not important. What is important is being obedient to God's calling, no matter how big or small, and to stay in tune with what He is leading me to do. I can't think of anything more important on Earth.

🕊 **How deliberate are you in the decisions you make each day? Do they point you towards or away from God?**

9/27/12

My hands and feet have been acting up over the last four days, especially my hands. They have a mild burning sensation, which is most noticeable in warm water. I went to my chemo appointment today and was discussing this with the doctor, and she decided it was time to "call it a day."

I did not see that coming. I figured we would at least do today, maybe at an even lower dose. But she told me she did not recommend it and listed all the reasons why. Each individual walks that fine line between getting the best cancer treatment and maintaining quality, day-to-day life unhindered by nerve damage. Yes, we want to fight the cancer, but we also want me to be able to tie my shoes, button buttons and zip zippers. Her example was to imagine if this morning's pain was at ten percent. After one more treatment, it wouldn't necessarily go to twenty percent, it could jump to ninety percent, and then it would be too late. We tried to get in as many chemo treatments as we could, but we have to stop before it's too late. She said that time is now.

I burst into tears, and I didn't even know why. It was just emotional. One part of it was disappointment that I didn't complete it, even though I knew from the beginning that most people don't, and this was the best thing for me. Another was shock, because I wasn't prepared to hear that. Another was relief that I was done with all of the sickness and difficulty of the medicines. It is strange to be disappointed and happy at the same time. I think there was even an element of sadness over knowing that I will no longer see my wonderful doctor and nurses that I have come to rely upon so heavily. I've gotten attached to those sweet people over there, helping save lives.

Now I'm sorting all that out, and I'm settling into the wonderful idea of regaining my strength and health to prepare for surgery. Goodbye steroids! I look like a puffer fish.

1. Have you ever experienced something that changed the way you look at things? What was it, and what changed?

2. Do you let the fear of what people might think, or their expectations of you, affect your actions in your day-to-day plans? If so, in what ways?

3. Do you let people affect your actions when God is calling you to

do something? If so, how?

4. The more time you spend with God, the more clearly you can hear Him. Is there something you can do to spend more time with Him to listen?

5. He will be as close to you as you allow Him to be. In your heart, do you acknowledge that He knows your every thought and intention, or do you try to keep Him at arm's length?

6. Not only is He near us, He is also where? Read Romans 8:9-11 and John 17:25-26.

7. How do Romans 8:14-17 describe your relationship with God? What does that mean to you personally?

8. How do we know that Jesus empathizes with our sufferings? See Philippians 2:5-8. What does this mean to you personally?

9. Read John 14:16-20.

    a. What are the two names used here for the Holy Spirit?

    b. Who cannot see Him or know Him?

    c. Where does He live?

    d. What does verse 26 say He will do?

    e. What does this mean to you personally?

10. Can you think of a time when you were upset or confused and knew you needed God, but didn't even know what to pray for? How will the Holy Spirit help? Read Romans 8:26-27.

11. What are you called in 1 Corinthians 3:16?

12. How can understanding how close you can be to God change the way you see Him, relate to Him and commune with Him?

Extend your study

Hebrews 4:13

Notes

NINE

God Is Not Bound

"Be joyful in hope, patient in affliction, faithful in prayer"
(Romans 12:12).

10/17/12

It's been a long time since I've written. Wow, almost a month. I have thought about writing, but I just haven't had much to say. I think I'm getting worn down. I'm tired. My brain doesn't work as well as I'd like it to. In every conversation, I find myself lost for words and unable to express what I'm trying to say. It's pretty frustrating, and I wonder what it's like for people who have known me for a long time. It must be weird for them to see the changes in me. I'm sure I'll get my brain back in time.

So I had a couple of scares over the past few weeks. This is frustrating because I was hoping to be "well" during this month off of chemo before surgery. First I battled a relentless headache. It was constant, and over-the-counter painkillers wouldn't help. I have some stronger stuff, but I can't use that all the time because I'm taking care of the kids. The headache lasted for over a week, so the doctor had me come in for a CT scan. I was thinking maybe I had a sinus infection or withdrawal symptoms from the steroids, but who knows? The doctor wanted to rule out that the cancer had spread to my brain or that I had some type of bleeding in my brain. Hmmm, I hadn't thought of those.

Sometimes I forget how serious my condition is. Now I have to think about death again. I trust that God has spoken and is taking care of me, but sometimes when a new complication arises, I can't help but think that maybe He is taking care of me as I leave this world, not like, making me well. Maybe He's keeping me at peace through my journey towards death. Maybe that's His answer, and I've just been assuming that He'll heal me and keep me here, but maybe His healing will come *through* death, when I will get my new body and be well forever. I don't think so, but I trust Him that either way everything will be ok.

The CT scan showed everything to be normal. Then I got another pain in my breast. This has happened before, but I never get any answers as to exactly what is causing it. There is a huge lump in there now, so of course I'm thinking the cancer must be growing back. Oh look, it's death, staring me in the face again. At this point, I can only go back to my wonderful verse, "My God is my rock, in Whom I take refuge." I need to trust God now like I trusted Him in the beginning, when I was so sick during chemo. I need to not tire of that, even though my body is tired.

I decided to spend some time with God in the Bible, and the first thing I was led to was this: "Keep your attention on Jesus Christ as risen from the dead and descended from David. This is according to my gospel. I suffer for it to the point of being bound like a criminal, but God's message is not bound" (2 Timothy 2:8-9, HCSB).

The way it fell on the page, I only saw, "Keep your attention on Jesus Christ" first. I stopped there because it hit me like a ton of bricks. I really let that sink in and remind me how I've gotten this far. It was by keeping my focus on Him, not on me, not on my diagnosis, not on my symptoms. I need to continue to look for things I can do right now to further His kingdom, even with my limited abilities. Maybe all I can do right now is write.

The second part about Paul "being bound like a criminal, but God's message is not bound," is very encouraging. It reminds me that, though I don't feel there is much I can do to serve Him right now, I will never know the ways He may be using my illness for His good. His works through me are not bound by my illness or my limited perception.

One small thing I *can* do is leave my shiny, bald head uncovered when I go out. I have found that as I go to the store or the kids' schools or wherever, it gets attention. People ask me about it, ask me how I'm feeling, even share that they or a family member has cancer too. It's a great opportunity for me to share my faith with complete strangers. I'm told that people are being affected by what I'm going through, so I just pray. I pray for all of those who are praying for me, and especially for the unbelievers who are watching me. I just know God is at work, and I am so thankful that He thinks I'm worthy of His use.

☙ What are some of your limitations, and how can God use them to further His kingdom?

So I saw a nurse practitioner today because my doctor wasn't in. She thinks the breast pain is an infection. I'm on an antibiotic and anxiously await its disappearance. If it doesn't go away, then I get to have the pleasure of another ultrasound and biopsy, but I'm not going think about that for now. One day at a time.

I love God. He has been so kind to me through all of this. I can't imagine what it's like where He lives.

11/1/12

So, the lump actually is cancer. Hmmm. I guess I'm one of the lucky few who gets a really fast-growing cancer. That's ok. My surgery is finally tomorrow, and my surgeon told me he will get it out of there. I can't wait. I can. not. wait! I'm excited to get going with the surgery and get this over with. My breast hurts so bad... it like radiates through my whole chest now. I can't wait to hear if the cancer is in my lymph nodes or not. I can't wait to hear if they got it all, if I need radiation, if I'll get reconstruction, all of that. Actually, cutting me open will answer lots of questions we've all had for a long time. Maybe that's what is so exciting – finally having answers, good or bad. At least we will know, for now anyway. Cancer can be such a sneaky little thing. It seems to just keep creeping up on people as they go about their business.

I suppose it will be a while before I write again. I really don't know how long the recovery will take. I have in my mind that it will be several weeks so that if it's any less, I will be pleasantly surprised. Bye for now.

(Ouch, if I leave it at that and die during surgery, people will use that last line at my funeral. Like, "Bye for now, see ya in Heaven!" I almost ended with, "See you on the other side!" but erased that because I meant on the other side of being unconscious in surgery, not like on the other side in eternity. Gosh, it's hard to write one last line that can't be used in an obituary. How about, I'll write more later after I recover from surgery and can call myself a survivor. Now THAT can't be used as my last words!)

1. Why do you think God allows us to experience difficulties and suffering?

2. What does Isaiah 55:8-9 say about God's ways?

3. Continue reading to Isaiah 55:10-11. What do you find encouraging about all of these verses (55:8-11), or what strikes you?

4. When trials last for long periods of time, we can get worn down. When we keep our attention on Christ, we can persevere. What does James 1:12 say about those who persevere?

5. What does Psalm 27:14 tell us? Is this easy or difficult for you in times of trouble?

What about when things are going well?

6. Sometimes what feels like suffering may be God's testing of our hearts. Read Psalm 66:10-12. What do you think it means to be "refined like silver?"

7. Read 2 Timothy 2:8-9 and 4:6-8. Paul left us a great example of keeping our faith, no matter what, until the very end. Are you living in such a way that you may one day make those same claims as in 4:7? How?

8. When believers go through hard times, the unbelieving world is watching. We can either complain and break down, or be examples of our Christian faith. Read Colossians 4:5. What does this verse tell us to do?

9. In Matthew 5:14-16, Jesus tells us that we are the light of the world. If we let His light shine before men in good times, and especially in bad, what may others see and do?

Extend your study

John 9:3

Psalm 42:5-11

Notes

TEN

A New Perspective

"If anyone speaks, he should do it as one speaking the very words of God. If anyone serves, he should do it with the strength God provides, so that in all things God may be praised through Jesus Christ. To Him be the glory and the power forever and ever. Amen"
(1 Peter 4:11).

11/24/12

I survived!

The surgery is over, and I've been at home recovering for the last few weeks. I can't wait to be well. I can't wait to have the freedom to do whatever I want to do instead of relying on other people. Everything went as planned though, and I am now cancer free.

I couldn't write for a long time because it was too difficult to hold my arms out in front of me to type. When I was finally able to type, everything that came to mind ended up being very emotional for me. I logged onto my site, but what I wanted to write wasn't very uplifting, and I don't want to spread negativity around. All I could think of was that I miss my life. I miss my life. That old life that was active and productive. I should view this as a good thing because it means that I am so far through treatment that I can allow myself to long for the life that is to come. I can't wait to start digging into projects around the house. It is so hard to sit here and not be able to do what I want to do.

But this is not a complaint. I am so thankful for where I am today. I am thankful that I have so much help that I can sit around or lie in bed or do whatever I need to do to get well. It's just that I am so close to having my health back that it's hard to wait.

I've been planning and imagining what that life will look like when I'm at full-strength. I pray that I will not forget how dependent I am on God. I pray I do not fill my life up so full that I can't spend time in prayer and in reading the Bible. I pray I do not take on so many commitments that I don't have the free time to indulge my children in what they want from me. What a blessing it has been to be completely removed from all obligations and duties and to be able to really look at what my life was and what I want it to be when I start really living again.

Right now, I am in a holding pattern. I am not in enough pain to stay in bed, but not well enough to accomplish much either. I guess I still just need to take one day at a time. Today was a good one.

I hope that each day of my new life is a celebration. I guess it will be what I make it.

☙ What are your first thoughts when you wake up each day, before you get out of bed?

1/12/13

I feel GOOD. I can't believe how many moments of the day I suddenly realize that nothing hurts. It's made me realize how long I wasn't well. Before I was diagnosed with cancer, I remember never feeling great. Something always hurt – my back, my arm, my legs – and I never had the energy I thought I should. I felt beat down and run down. I know they say that cancer doesn't cause all of these symptoms, but in my body, for whatever reason, I felt bad overall. Now that my cancer is gone, my body feels great. I feel normal! Well, my new normal. I guess I am a bit deformed, but I don't care. It's just a part of my life – a part I don't think I would change if I could.

It sounds crazy, but my experience through cancer has been the most cherished time in my life with God. I used to pray that I would get to see Him in some tangible way, and that is exactly what happened. He used the bad, my illness, for good, just as He says He will in Romans 8:28a: "And we know that in all things God works for the good of those who love him." That time was sacred, and I do not use that word lightly. It changed my life. It changed who I am. It changed my perspective.

For one thing, I was grocery shopping yesterday and actually stopped to smell the roses in the flower department. Then I had to laugh because I realized I was living the cliché. But that's just it. I cherish each moment I have because I am now so thankful to have them. It's not because I am clinging to this life in this world. I am still excited for what eternity holds, but I am so excited that God told me *yes* and granted me the time to raise my children.

It has changed our whole family. We all seem to appreciate each other more. We all help each other more and work more like a team. This is probably how God designed us to function, but we're always so concerned about our own needs that we tend to overlook others'.

So, this cancer has been a gift. While it was very difficult – I do not mean to downplay that by any means – more good than bad has come from it. It was so great a struggle, and I had such a deep dependency on God, that I got to see very clearly how close He is to each of us.

I guess that's why the word "sacred" comes to mind to describe that time. When I look back, half of it is just a blur of lying in bed, taking pills and riding in the car. It doesn't feel like that many months have gone by. The other half was experiencing God Himself. I cherish the experiences I had with Him, and still have. I guess that's the part that feels like a gift. I still feel that close to Him. I still feel Him right here, and I hear Him so clearly. I don't ever want to move from this spot.

That might be one reason it has been difficult for me to get back involved in my life; I don't want to leave this place. But as more time goes by and I still have this closeness to Him, I am realizing that as I move, He is moving with me. I don't have to sit still for fear of leaving the shadow of His wing. He wants me to go on and be a useful tool for Him, and He will never leave me. Deuteronomy 31:6 says, "Be strong and courageous. Do not be afraid or terrified because of them, for the Lord your God goes with you; he will never leave you nor forsake you." I guess I used to read that verse and sort of picture God nearby, but He is so much closer than nearby! He is all-consuming. He is all up in my space! I praise Him for opening my eyes. "Therefore, since we are receiving a kingdom that cannot be shaken, let us be thankful, and so worship God acceptably with reverence and awe, for our 'God is a consuming fire' " (Hebrews 12:28-29).

1. Have you ever *literally* stopped to smell the flowers in the floral department? Pulled the car over to gaze at an amazing sunset or rainbow? Or just slowed down enough to take pleasure in the wonderful things God has given us here to enjoy? Describe here.

2. If money, time and daily responsibilities were no issue, and you could do anything you wanted to do with your life, what would it be?

3. Now, within the constraints of finances and time, if you could completely step out of your obligations, and then step back in, what would you prioritize and add back in? What would you cut out?

4. Do you let factors like money and time hold you back from doing the things you feel God calling you to do? If so, why? What are they keeping you from?

5. We like to think that we are in control in all situations. When we lose our health, we realize just how helpless we really can be. Has there been a time in your life when you felt helpless? Explain.

6. Has God ever unexpectedly met your needs, taken care of you, or revealed His presence to you in some way? If so, how?

7. Review your answers to questions 5 and 6. How can these be used as a part of your testimony?

8. Do you tend to picture God as just "nearby?" James 4:8a says, "Come near to God and He will come near to you." What does this tell us about His accessibility?

9. While we can be in such close relationship with Him, we must not

get too comfortable and forget who He is.   What do Hebrews 12:28-29 remind us?

10. We cannot sit idly in the comfort of His closeness. We need to grow and seek wisdom and guidance, then go into the world and do His work. We like to make big plans on our own and think that we have our futures all mapped out. In reality, none of us knows what the future holds, and no amount of planning can control every aspect of our lives. We must align our will with His and let Him teach us how to follow. Then He will lead us to joy and peace and freedom. Read James 4:13-15. How ought we to live according to verse 15?

11. We must praise Him and be in reverent awe of Him. He will be with us and in us. He says He will never leave us, and in Him, all things are possible. We do not know the number of our days, so we must live each as if it is our last. What is God calling you to do in your life right now?

Extend your study

Romans 12:1-2

Notes

Pray for God to open your eyes so that you may see Him more clearly than ever before, and experience the wonder of His love even more intimately each and every day that He gives you. Look for His blessings in all circumstances, and you will surely find them.

He does use ALL things for good, even cancer.

Made in the USA
Charleston, SC
31 December 2013